I0816793

The True and Lucky LIFE OF A TURTLE

Written by SY MONTGOMERY Illustrated by MATT PATTERSON

CLARION BOOKS
An Imprint of HarperCollinsPublishers

THIS IS FIRE CHIEF—a forty-two-pound common snapping turtle who is strong and brave. He's as old as your grandparents and could still be the ruler of his pond when *you're* a grandparent, too.

But when Fire Chief was born, he was almost as small as a quarter—

so small that even a fish could swallow him.

As a baby, he had to spend most of his time hiding. . . .

Fire Chief has been lucky, though, and has had help from human friends during his many adventures.

Without their help, we couldn't tell his incredible story.

It all began one rainy spring evening, about sixty years ago. A scaly, shelled visitor hauled herself up a sandy New England hill. She had left her pond and walked for many hours to reach this south-facing slope. Here, under the cover of twilight, she dug a hole with her strong back legs and laid more than a dozen precious eggs the size of Ping-Pong balls. She carefully covered them back up with sand and then left to return to her pond. The warm summer sun would do the rest.

Three months later, the smooth sand exploded with life: The baby snapping turtles had hatched!

They didn't know how lucky they already were, for many nests get destroyed. Skunks and raccoons dig up the eggs to eat them. Drought can dry them out. Ants and flies invade the nest. People and dogs sometimes disturb the eggs, too.

Though lucky, these babies still had a difficult journey ahead. They had to find a pond, and each baby turtle had to face many dangers while getting there.

Hungry foxes and coyotes might find them. Birds like crows could swoop in for a turtle feast. Snakes might swallow them whole. Even a chipmunk will eat a little turtle!

Brave baby Fire Chief walked down the hill and crossed a country road. On tiny, clawed feet smaller than pencil erasers, he plodded through fields. He passed a house and walked through a yard.

A quarter mile away, he found a small pond shaped like a heart.
It was the water supply for a brand-new fire station.

And it was perfect.

Fire Chief quickly hid among the cattails, pickerelweed, and lily pads.

Frogs and fish couldn't see him. He hid from the heron who visited. Not even the firefighters in the firehouse knew he was there . . .

. . . until, years later, someone spotted the snapping turtle basking on a log. Fire Chief was now ten years old. He was nearly a foot long—big enough that almost no one could eat him. He was no longer afraid. He was the king of his pond. What a lucky turtle!

Every fall, some of the firefighters would see Fire Chief crawl out of the heart-shaped pond and walk across the road to a larger pond. This was a better place for him to spend the winter, buried in the mud. The crew would see him again each spring, when he came back to his summer pond—a better place to find the fish, insects, and plants that he loved to eat.

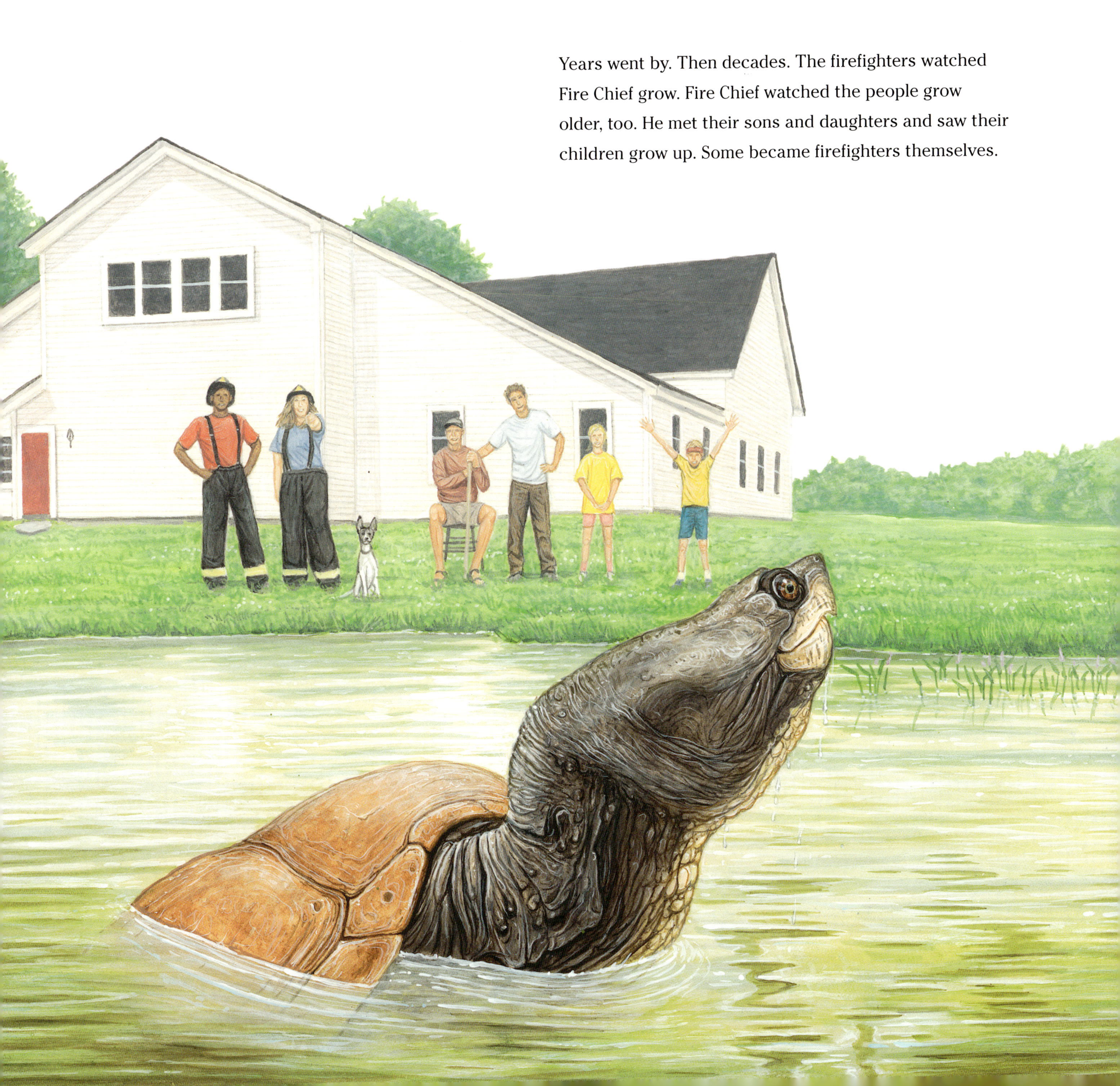

Years went by. Then decades. The firefighters watched Fire Chief grow. Fire Chief watched the people grow older, too. He met their sons and daughters and saw their children grow up. Some became firefighters themselves.

The town was also changing. There were more houses, more people, more cars. The dirt road separating Fire Chief's summer and winter ponds was paved with asphalt and painted with a double yellow line. The country lane had become a state highway filled with fast cars.

And then one day, Fire Chief was *un*lucky.

49278

A passerby called for help. Badly hurt, Fire Chief crawled back to his heart-shaped pond. The firefighters gathered nearby, worried about their friend. But they were too afraid to pick him up. Fire Chief was now a very big snapping turtle—he weighed as much as a lawn mower—and most people, even brave firefighters, are afraid of them.

But not the people at Turtle Rescue League.

Natasha and Alexxia arrived in their turtle ambulance. They launched their kayak in the pond. Alexxia dived in—and came up with Fire Chief in her arms.

Back at their turtle hospital, Natasha and Alexxia cleaned Fire Chief's wounds. They patched his broken shell. The accident had also injured his back legs. But snapping turtles are strong and brave—and sometimes lucky. "Give him time," Natasha said.

"We never give up on a turtle!" Alexxia agreed.

When his wounds began to heal,

Fire Chief was moved to a big hospital tank.

Thanks to the good care at the rescue league, Fire Chief's broken shell was on the mend. But he still could barely move his back legs. To help strengthen them, Natasha and Alexxia made a plan: Volunteers would help him exercise to build muscle and flexibility. Sometimes other injured turtles joined him in the Turtle Garden.

They built him a special wheelchair so he could exercise indoors year-round—even on the slippery floors.

Seasons passed and Fire Chief's confidence grew. With the volunteers' help, his legs became stronger.

But were they strong enough to get him across the busy highway between his summer and winter ponds? Would he be fast enough to beat the whizzing cars?

Is any turtle?

Alexxia and Natasha feared the big turtle's legs would never fully recover. But Fire Chief's friends came up with a solution:

They dug him a pond far from any road.

They planted it with cattails and pickerelweed and lily pads.
And they filled it with water—with a shallow end and a deep end, so he could choose just the right spot to spend both summer and winter.

Now Fire Chief is the king of his own pond again—
with a little help from his human friends.
What a lucky turtle!

Sy and Matt in Fire Chief's pond, in Matt's backyard. (Photo by Susie Spikol)

THIS IS A TRUE STORY

FIRE CHIEF NOW LIVES with the artist who illustrated this book, right up the street from the author who wrote it.

Matt and Sy met Fire Chief when they began volunteering with Turtle Rescue League in the spring of 2020. The Chief had been recovering there since his accident in October 2018. Depending on the season, founders Alexxia Bell and Natasha Nowick may care for anywhere between 250 and 1,000 injured, sick, or abandoned pet turtles in their home in Southbridge, Massachusetts. Many of them were hit by cars, just like Fire Chief. Many of them are common snapping turtles, just like him.

We can't be sure it was a rainy night when the egg that hatched Fire Chief was laid—back then, Sy was a little girl growing up in another state, and Matt hadn't even been born yet. But this is likely; many mother turtles prefer to lay their eggs on wet evenings. Rain softens the ground and helps them dig their nests. And we don't know for sure if it was a south-facing slope where his nest was dug all those years ago, but turtles often choose a spot like that, knowing the warm sun will help incubate their eggs. We do think we know where he hatched, though. When we visited the heart-shaped pond, we were able to find the place his mother, and many other turtle mothers since then, almost certainly considered ideal for nesting. It's about a quarter mile away from his pond. And we were able to see exactly where Fire Chief's accident happened, when he was trying to cross to his hibernation pond, and where Alexxia and Natasha launched their kayak to rescue him.

ABOUT SNAPPING TURTLES

MANY PEOPLE ARE AFRAID OF SNAPPING TURTLES. They shouldn't be. Snapping turtles do not attack people or pets. They mainly eat insects, worms, and fish. Much of what big adult snappers eat is already dead. They are like the vultures of the pond, cleaning up dead fish and other carrion. Without them, their ponds would become a stinky mess.

There are two kinds of snapping turtles in North and South America: the common snapping turtle and the larger, more southern, alligator snapping turtle. These species are not endangered. But like turtles almost everywhere, their numbers are dwindling. One reason is our busy roads—roads that were not busy, or were not even there, for most of turtles' existence on this earth. (Turtles arose at the same time as the dinosaurs!)

Lots of animals eat baby snapping turtles and their eggs. In fact, 90 percent of snapper eggs are eaten by predators before they hatch! Only one out of a hundred hatchlings survive long enough to mate and lay eggs themselves. But once a snapping turtle gets as big as Fire Chief, he might be able to live for another hundred years or more.

Snapping turtles only bite when they are afraid of being attacked. They might even snap by mistake at someone who is trying to rescue them or help them cross the street.

There are several ways to safely move a snapping turtle:

If it's a small snapper who will fit in your hands, you can move him just like any other turtle. Calmly lift him by the edges of the shell. Keep your fingers away from his mouth.

If it's a large, old snapper like the Chief, you can get the turtle to step onto a floor mat from a car, the flat part of a shovel, or an unfolded cardboard box. Then you can drag him across the street to safety. The safest way is to pull the mat or shovel with the turtle on it facing backward. Then spin it around once you've crossed so the turtle is facing the direction he was going—not back into oncoming traffic.

If the snapper is injured, you need to get him into a box to bring to a rehabilitator. Even very large snappers can be safely lifted. Calmly and quietly approach the turtle from the back. Slide your palm under the turtle's belly to pick him up. You can hold the base (not the tip) of the tail to keep him steady. Never hold a turtle upside down by the tail—this can damage their spinal cord. If you wear gloves, even better: You won't get scratched by his back toenails.

If you are afraid to pick up the turtle, you can put a box over him, to protect him from flies and predators, and call for a police or animal control officer to help you. Stay with the turtle until help comes.

Fire Chief and Matt enjoy a swim. (Photo by Erin Patterson)

RESOURCES

Found an injured turtle? Get the patient to a rehabilitator, fast, for the very specialized care turtles need. Here's how to find a turtle rehabilitator near you:

www.nwrawildlife.org/page/Found_Injured_Wildlife
www.humanesociety.org/resources/how-find-wildlife-rehabilitator

Although some turtles are common, of the more than 350 different kinds around the world, over 60 percent of them are in danger of extinction—because their homes are being destroyed, because of global climate change, because of an illegal trade in turtles, and because of the same dangers Fire Chief faced. Turtle Survival Alliance is dedicated to zero turtle extinctions—in fact, that's their motto. Find out how they're saving turtles and how you can help by visiting **turtlesurvival.org**.

Or write to them at:
Turtle Survival Alliance
5900 Core Road, Suite 504
North Charleston, SC 29406

And if you would like to support or volunteer with Natasha and Alexxia at Turtle Rescue League in Southbridge, Massachusetts, here's how to reach them: **turtlerescueleague.org**.

To everyone who has ever rescued a turtle, and to all those who work to conserve wetlands, reduce the dangers of roads, and advance the day that no turtle species will be threatened with extinction.

Clarion Books is an imprint of HarperCollins Publishers.

The True and Lucky Life of a Turtle

For information address HarperCollins Children's Books, a division of HarperCollins Publishers, 195 Broadway, New York, NY 10007.
www.harpercollinschildrens.com

Library of Congress Control Number: 2024948562
ISBN 978-0-06-332516-6

The artist used a funny grip on the paintbrush to create the illustrations for this book.
Typography by Cara Llewellyn
25 26 27 28 29 RRDSEA 10 9 8 7 6 5 4 3 2 1

First Edition